D1107601

This book is a special gift

To:

Tammy & Jeff

From:

Deanna, Toty & Hage.

Date:

November 9, 2001

Message:

Happy Anniversary

365 Things that every

Couple

should know

Murray Janson

Originally published by Christian Publishing Company under the title *365 Dinge wat elke paartjie moet weet* © 1995

This edition published by Christian Art Gifts
PO Box 1599, Vereeniging, 1930, South Africa

© 2000

Translated by Linda Beukes

Cover designed by Christian Art Gifts

Unless otherwise indicated, all Scripture quotations are taken from the *Holy Bible*: New International Version. Copyright © 1973, 1978, 1984 by International Bible Society. Used by permission of Zondervan Publishing House. All rights reserved.

Printed in Singapore

ISBN 1-86852-654-2

00 01 02 03 04 05 06 07 08 09 · 10 9 8 7 6 5 4 3 2 1

365 Things that every

Couple

should know

*I*ndex

Foreword

How should marriage partners read this book? Anyway you please. If I may, I would like to suggest the following: read one proverb every day, and practise it throughout the year, and think about it during the day. Of course, the ideal is that each partner should check to see whether you are applying it! If all of them, or quite a number are read consecutively, it soon becomes dull and boring. With that I am not trying to say that each of the 365 things is a wonderful proverb, which no one else has ever thought of! And yet I hope that it will mean something to many couples.

I pray that you may have 365 days of happiness, multiplied by the number of years you still have left together!

~ *Murray Janson* ~

CONSIDERATION (1-9)

Be considerate towards your partner throughout the year in every possible way – just like during your engagement – and don't do anything that would hurt your partner.

1

that the only way to demonstrate what your love is made of, is to always be considerate towards your partner.

2

your partner's shoe size.

3

how to cure your partner's headache with a dose of love.

4

that "please" and "thank you" are not
words that only children should say.

5

that when you are exhausted, you
are actually revitalised by
showing an interest in your partner.

6

how strong tenderness is.

7

that every act of decency and
etiquette shown to others is merely a show if you don't show it
to your partner in the first place.

8

that you should treat your
partner in the same way that you
would like your partner to treat you.

9

that other people should
also see that you are
considerate towards each other.

COMMUNICATION (10-17)

*One would think that all marriage partners
communicate effectively, and yet poor
communication (or lack of communication) is
the single most common problem in marriages
today.*

10

that the most important part of
communication is listening.

<u>11</u>

that God has – definitely not
by chance! – given you
two ears and **one** mouth.

<u>12</u>

that you should learn to listen
actively to what your partner has
to say – and especially to how he
feels, and that touching is an
important way of communicating.

<u>13</u>

that the television should
sometimes be switched
off and the communication
process be switched on.

14

that love means you should sometimes
talk – and sometimes keep quiet.

15

that you should learn to keep
those words that you really want
to say the most to yourself.

16

how to also understand your
partner's body language –
and interpret it positively.

17

that you should just dare to talk to
each other in the beginning –
because every time you come closer to
what you really feel and mean to say.

~ 15 ~

MARITAL BLISS REQUIRES HARD WORK (18-28)

The romantic conception that once two people are married, the line "And they lived happily ever after," will automatically apply, is a myth. You cannot have something if you don't work hard to obtain it.

18

that the most common mistake made in marriage is to think that once the wedding is over, marital bliss automatically follows.

19

that God has given you nuts, but you have to crack them open yourself.

20

that you should already
on your wedding day con-
centrate on behaving in
exactly the same manner
towards each other as
you did during the months
preceding the wedding.

21

that when it comes to love,
two halves don't make a whole.

22

that there is nothing more
exciting than having a
big goal, working hard at
it and eventually succeeding.

23

that the process you are busy with in order to achieve success is more important than the success itself.

24

that working on a marriage is not hard labour, but trying to make your partner happy brings you joy and happiness.

25

that she doesn't have to make his clothes, and that he doesn't have to wash the floors for her every day, but that she should always be prepared to pick up his clothes from the floor, and he should rather give her a back rub than a back chat.

26:

that happy marriages are
made in heaven, but are
realised on earth through actions.

27

that if you are inclined to forget
your anniversary, you should even
get a company to phone you that
morning, just to remember it –
if you claim to love your partner.

28

that any two people could
be happily married if they
wanted to be, the more so when
they have chosen each other.

SPACE IN YOUR CLOSENESS (29-42)

Getting married to each other doesn't imply that you now own each other, and that you lose your own personality. No, you should now more than ever free your partner to be him or herself.

29

that you should still allow
enough space in your closeness.

30

that you should look at your
partner in such a way that
the look in your eyes doesn't
tie him to the past, but
frees him for the future.

31

that it is unnecessary for two
people to always agree on everything.

32

that the perfect partner is one who
doesn't expect the other to be perfect.

33

that if you want to try to tie down
your partner, it always becomes a
prison he wants to escape from.

34

that it is your biggest duty and
privilege to help your partner to
develop into the person God has
really intended him or her to be.

35

that only when you have each
become completely free within yourselves, you really
have a meaningful relationship.

36

that instead of trying to
change your partner into
the right person, you should
rather try to be the right
person for your partner.

37

that if you deny your partner the
right to be a person in his own
right, you are also denying yourself.

38

a good marriage gives both partners
the right and space to grow, and
to have some perspectives you
wouldn't have had if you were alone.

39

that failure is an event, not a person.

40

that the biggest and most important
room a person should lay claim
to is room for improvement.

41

that you should set your partner free
with this golden sticker attached to
him or her: you may sometimes fail.

42

that both should strive to be
honest without being insulting,
to be frank without being subver-
sive, to share without controlling,
to love without possessing.

UNSELFISHNESS (43-50)

*Love isn't naturally unselfish. On the contrary,
natural love is extremely selfish! Therefore we
should constantly be converted in our love:
converted back to unselfishness!*

43

that the great command says you
should love your neighbour as you
love yourself, and that marriage is
the greatest training-school God has
given us to practise this command.

44

that if you should only spend
a quarter of the sympathy,
excuse and defence you
claim for yourself on your
partner, the sun will almost
rise in the west this evening –
over your wonderful marriage.

45

that in reality you only
own and keep ... that
which you give away.

46

that if you constantly nag
and fuss and worry, you
have already decided that
your marriage shouldn't work.

<u>47</u>

that everything you sa-
crifice for the sake of
your partner will later on
be the most valuable to you.

<u>48</u>

that only once you've
removed the beam (which
Jesus was nailed to!) from
your own eye, will you
really be able to kiss the small
motes from your partner's eye.

<u>49</u>

that even if you have ten de-
grees or diplomas or certifi-
cates, you still have to learn
how to lose in your marriage.

<u>50</u>

that the greatest gift you can
receive from a person is being
able to give a little bit of yourself.

CONFLICT (51-56)
*The thing which will most surely crop up in
your marriage is differences, which (if we don't
prevent it) could easily lead to quarrels and
enormous conflict.*

<u>51</u>

that having problems is no
shame, but that it is a shame
if you don't try to solve them.

<u>52</u>

that the winner of an
argument is actually the loser.

<u>53</u>

that you could win the
argument, but lose your marriage.

<u>54</u>

that it's much better looking at
what is right, than who is right.

<u>55</u>

that if one is sorting out
conflict, it's much better
saying, "I feel," than "you are."

<u>56</u>

that it is all right to
agree to disagree.

LOVE (57-78)

As far as love is concerned, we all share in the Hollywood belief that love is merely a feeling, which can "unfortunately" sooner or later disappear.

<u>57</u>

that a day without saying
"I love you" is a day wasted
and if you don't tell your
partner that you love him
or her, you won't act
out your love either.

<u>58</u>

that conflicts as such are not
so important and are part
of every marriage. They do,
however, become problems
when used as ammunition.

59

that love is a verb, and that it is
therefore not important how much
love you feel for your partner, but with
how much love you shower him or her.

60

that the Hollywood romances
are not filmed in the real world.

61

that God's love for your
partner contains no conditions.

62

that love isn't something that happens
to you, but something you have to
work at so that it happens every day.

63

that a great lover isn't someone who jumps from one
partner to the next (dogs
also do that), but some-
one who loves one partner
for the rest of his or her life.

64

that love is a very humble
matter, which serves its
food in earthly vessels, but
which brings heavenly bliss
to those who share in it.

65

that love exposes its feet, even if
the road hits them with fists.

66

that the quiet smile of love
transforms the poorest
house into a home.

67

that love is changing a baby's nappy.

68

that love means always
sticking to your choice.

69

that love means never ever again
comparing after the wedding day.

70

that every misunderstanding
is basically a lack of love.

71

that our natural sympathy (before the
Lord changes us) is as thin as the
slot of the collection box through
which we push our meagre coin.

72

that loving someone means admiring
the best in him or her, and balancing
out the rest with your own weaknesses.

73

that marriage is really the only
place where love is truly a reality.

74

that love means today being what you
promised yesterday to be tomorrow.

75

that every person is only
as great as his or her love.

76

that love must be cherished
and fed, nurtured and
sweetened, elevated
and enriched, nursed
and warmed – otherwise it is
impoverished and pines away.

77

that giving love and receiving love
means seeing the sun day and night.

78

that love is not an emotion,
but is everything you have
experienced with someone.

SELF-IMAGE (79-96)

*One of the privileges, but also duties of a
marriage is that we should build and strengthen
our partner's self-image. And amazingly, by
doing this, our own self-image is also greatly
improved.*

79

how to make your partner feel great.

80

that everybody needs
somebody to give you a new
and better image of yourself.

81

that we should all learn to
disregard one great mis-
conception: that we believe
deep down inside that we
should first become perfect
before we can become human.

82

that self-worth does not lie in
what you have but in what you are.

83

that except for the bathroom
mirror, someone else should
also become your mirror –
where you can always see yourself looking better than you feel.

84

that everyone who has a
true friend and partner
doesn't really need a mirror.

85

how to celebrate
your partner's victories.

86

that every person
loves to feel important.

87

that by running your partner
down, you are only showing
that you don't know what it means
to build your future together.

88

that you should swell with
pride when introducing
your partner to someone.

89

that she loves hearing how
beautiful she is, and he loves
hearing how handsome he is.

90

that your partner is extremely precious.

91

to only say good things
about your partner in his
or her absence – or presence.

92

that complete acceptance
of your partner forms the foun-
dation on which you should
build each other's self-image –
if not, your marriage is built
on the loose sand of emotions.

93

that you should have
a hopeful perspective on
your partner's negative past.

94

that people can survive
the storms of life if they
turn to each other
instead of attacking each
other during these storms.

95

that the most important human
need is being acknowledged.

96

that your self-image grows to the
extent that you build your partner's.

CHILDREN (97-108)

*Children don't ask a lot from their parents,
only love. And love doesn't imply feelings, but
acts: attention and involvement and sacrifice,
and, when it may become necessary, even
opposing your child.*

97

that a good and happy marriage
is the only real education
you can give your children.

98

that you should promote
a positive image of your
partner in your children –
because you love your children.

99

that whether you want to or
not, whether you want
others to see it or not,
you bear the stamp of
your parents within yourself.

100

that children and parents become
like the best or the worst
things they give each other.

<u>101</u>

that children have the right to be
heard, to be children, and (just
like their parents) to be imperfect.

<u>102</u>

that children actually learn by
example; therefore the best
way a parent can influence a
child is by behaving in a way they
would like to see the child behave.

<u>103</u>

that children can all too
easily become the candles
that are created by people,
in order to light the flame
that never burnt in their own lives.

104

that nothing ever prevents a
child more from becoming
him or herself than trying to be
something that he or she isn't.

105

that children have the right to
be loved and hugged, sometimes even for no other reason
than merely being within arm's
length away from the parent.

106

that children have the right not to be
spoilt – because spoiling a child is
actually a way of rejecting a child.

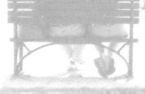

107

that parents have the right to a
degree of peace and quiet.

108

that they ought to behave so
lovingly towards their children-
in-law that they will be glad to
see them arrive – and not depart.

SEX (109-125)

*We are inclined to confuse sex and love. In
reality sex is, however, merely one way of
communicating love.*

109

that making love doesn't necessarily
mean sex, and having sexual
contact doesn't always mean love.

<u>110</u>✪

that love should also
be given and made real
without sex and passion.

<u>111</u>

that "making love"
last of all means sex.

<u>112</u>

that sex starts in the
morning when you
treat your partner well.

<u>113</u>

about the simple
intimacy of holding hands.

114

that sex shouldn't be something
you have to want, but something
you want to give your partner.

115

that sex won't make emotional
and other problems disappear.

116

that sex is not a way
of making peace, but
that the peace-making
should precede it.

117

that if the man loves his wife in
the kitchen and in the TV room,
she will love him in the bedroom.

118

that the foreplay to sex should be
continued into the afterplay of life.

119

that if there is a sexual
problem in the marriage,
it is usually more of a
relational problem
than a lack of technique.

120

that you can study and master
the most exotic techniques
and positions, but if you don't
know how to win your partner
over with the right words, you
might as well save yourself the effort.

121

that if sex becomes a matter
of course and habit, your
partner becomes a mere
object to alleviate stress.

122

that the best book to read
about sex is the chronicles
of your partner's feelings.

123

that you don't have to be
ashamed to call those things
by name that God wasn't ashamed
about when He created them.

124

that as far as sex is concerned,
you are not in the sphere of that
which is sinful and chaotic, but
that which is still in the sphere of
God, and that you therefore
don't have to have a guilty
conscience about it, and have
the full right to say "yes" to this.

125

that sex without a
relationship of love is harlotry.

COMPLIMENTS (126-130)

During your engagement you often gave your partner compliments. What a shame if you stop this after your wedding! Marriage partners definitely have an even greater need for compliments than engaged couples.

<u>126</u>

that one compliment a day
means that your partner is
living below the breadline.

<u>127</u>

that you ought to write your
criticism in the sand and
your compliments on marble.

<u>128</u>

that giving compliments is a
wonderful cure for deafness.

<u>129</u>

that people are inclined to
become that which you inspire
them to become, and not that which
you reproach them for not being.

<u>130</u>

that as long as you can admire
and love, you will remain young.

FUN (131-143)

Life is something that should be tackled zealously. That does not, however, mean that there is not also room for wonderful moments of fun in marriage. Laughter heals.

<u>131</u>

that your marriage should have
far more dreams than nightmares.

<u>132</u>

that showering together
saves a lot of water.

133

that taking a bath together,
means only having one bath to
clean – and a fresh relationship.

134

how important it is to have
your own vocabulary that
no one else understands.

135

that you should always be
ready to surprise your partner.

136

that you could be so busy taking
care of the future, that you
don't notice and experience
the good things about today.

137

that if you are truly serious about God (and not yourself) you could enjoy a life that is carefree and filled with large amounts of healthy fun.

138

that if you cannot sometimes laugh spontaneously and heartily, you will prematurely (and per-manently) become as sour as vinegar.

139

that a marriage without regular portions of shared fun will quickly die due to demureness, false seriousness and self-interest.

<u>140</u>

that God not only prescribes his
commandments, but also some fun.

<u>141</u>

how to spoil your partner out
of this world (and into heaven).

<u>142</u>

that spoiling your partner,
won't spoil him or her.

<u>143</u>

that if you can no longer produce
any pleasant and joyful moments
with your partner, you have no
sense of humour or neighbourly love.

GROWTH (144-158)
Growth means life. Therefore we should take care that our marriage grows and develops, becomes riper and flourishes in all respects.

144

that you ought to be more inclined to look for solutions, rather than being problem-oriented.

145

that a growing marriage will carry you through the difficult days of old age.

146

that you cling to your bad habits, because you don't like risking growth – and also to try to explain away your failures.

<u>147</u>

that growth can only take place when
you discover that you don't have to or
want to remain the way you are now.

<u>148</u>

that successful relationships
don't happen by chance.

<u>149</u>

that if you and your partner hug
each other regularly, you
won't bug each other later on.

150 ✧

that growth means that you
sometimes cross a boundary
that you will never return to.

151

that the wastebasket in
your home should be
filled regularly – by throwing your old, rigid opinions,
and parts of your old,
wrongful ego away in it.

152

that if you do not grow and
become mature, you will always
be inclined to seek the excitement
of a new relationship and the
discovery of another person.

153

that "new" according to the dictionary
means "of recent origin" or "invented,
acquired or experienced recently or
now for the first time" or "unfamiliar
or strange." Therefore you should
regularly ask yourself: What about your
life and attitude towards your partner
is of recent origin, or recently experienced for the first time, or unfamiliar?

154

that the ideal marriage relationship allows
both partners to keep on growing into
a new person whom the other can
fall in love with over and over again.

155

that you should be able to depend on
your partner's love and support, so that
in the process you will be allowed to grow
into the person you really ought to be.

156.

that if you don't belong
to yourself, you cannot
belong to anyone else either.

157

that in marriage and in life
you only grow to the
extent that you promote
your partner's growth.

158

that growing means changing,
changing means maturing,
maturing means allowing God to
recreate you over and over again.

APOLOGISING (159-168)

Relationships cannot survive if both of us don't regularly apologise for our blunders and slips, as well as for our horrible mistakes and shortcomings. It's the butter on the bread of marriage.

159

that it is much nicer forgiving a
blunder than kicking up a fuss about it.

160

that the words "I'm sorry"
invites spring into your marriage.

161

that you should always
try to apologise first.

16:2

that two times two in marriage
equals a hundred – because if
both partners are prepared to just
place two percent of the guilt on
his or her own account, matters will
often be one hundred percent right.

16:3

that if you jump into the
waves of remorse, you will
stand even less of a chance
of sinking than in the Dead Sea.

16:4

that the only way to truly
end an argument is with
the words "I apologise."

165

that saying that you forgive but can't forget only means that you don't really want to forgive.

166

that making someone beg on hands and knees for forgiveness is at least as bad as the mistake he or she has made.

167

that guilt is a word, but forgiveness is a Person.

168

that one knows that the Spirit of the Lord lives in your heart when you start apologising and forgiving.

GRATITUDE (169-174)

People often feel that gratitude is a sign of weakness and dependence. The truly independent and strong person is always a grateful person. Besides, who of us is not dependent?

169

that you regularly ought
to write a lovely letter of
gratitude and appreciation
to your partner – and mean it.

170

that you should especially
thank your partner
on your day of success.

171

that just as wrong as it is to point to your partner to excuse yourself, it is Christ-like (and wonderful) to point to your partner when you have achieved success.

172

that only gratitude can make you relax, and that the same gratitude can enable you to put in some effort.

173

that Paul's prayer was answered when he started seeing the thorn in his side as a blessing.

174

that if you aren't often grateful
for your partner, you have
allowed a piece of your life to die.

PRAYER (175-182)

*How can I hope for my marriage partner to be
happy, strong and full of hope, and be able to
stay with me, if I don't pray for him or her every
day?*

175

that if you haven't prayed for
your partner today, it means
that you are prepared to throw
your partner to the dogs.

176

to often pray the following: Thy will be
done in our marriage, as it is in heaven.

177

that people don't live like slaves under a sultan, but that Christians are God's free citizens – with a right to vote.

178

that God allows our prayers to erase the dotted lines of his plans for us.

179

that God allows the order in his house to be disturbed when the prodigal son enters like a prayer.

180

that you are servants of God in obedience, children of God in faith, but friends of God in prayer.

181

that you should be demanding,
yes, even audacious in prayer, for
the very reason of being modest.

182

that the Bible says that if the
faithful pray, the heavens fall
silent for half an hour (cf. Rev. 8:1).

FAITH (183-193)

*Marriage is a gift from God. Therefore people
can't really get married without faith in God.
And believing in God especially means doing
in your marriage what God expects from his
children.*

183

that you would rather jump off the
highest top of the temple than
apologising and settling a quarrel.

184

that Christians should much
rather confess than accuse.

185

that marriage is God's training-
school, where you truly learn
how to become a Christian.

186

that you only love God to
the extent that you love you
marriage partner (cf. 1 Jn. 4:20).

<u>187</u>

that if you aren't a Christian in
your marriage, you cannot and
will not be one anywhere else.

<u>188</u>

that religion in your marriage means
understanding a little (and often
being aware of the fact) that you
are part of the miracle we call life –
with which God creates and blesses us.

<u>189</u>

that a person without an
openness to God and an
awareness that He exists
has not yet progressed
further than an animal.

190

that faith means that you start
thinking about the secret of your
origin, and the mystery of your future.

191

that you may love each other – only
because the love of God comes to kiss
you on the mouth at Christmas-time.

192

that disbelief still seeks
arguments that look very believable.

193

that true faith means still being
able to hear a bit of music and
song amid the noise of daily life
and the clatter of the darkest night.

THE TEN COMMANDMENTS
FOR MARRIAGE (194-203)

*If the Bible would have given us ten command-
ments for marriage, what would they have
been? Maybe some of the following would
have been included.*

194

that the first commandment for marriage may have been something
like this: You may not automatically
assume that your marriage will
succeed, you should work at it –
by especially working at it yourself.

195

that the second commandment for
marriage probably could have been:
You may not have any ideal image of a
marriage partner, and constantly try to
change your partner into that image.

196

that the third commandment may have
said: Six days you should labour, and
do all your work, but you will have to
find some time in between to spend
with your partner and your family.

197

that the fourth commandment of
the ten commandments for marriage
could have sounded as follows:
You should not commit adultery.

198

that the fifth commandment could
have been formulated as follows:
Honour your mother-in-law
and your father-in-law just
as much as your own parents.

199

that we may have stated commandment number six as: Discuss
your differences and solve them.

200

that the seventh commandment
could have been: Always forgive
each other for everything.

201

that the eighth marriage
commandment could have
said: You may never forget to
pray for your marriage partner.

202

that the ninth command-
ment of the ten com-
mandments for marriage
may be formulated as
follows: You should
love the Lord your God.

203

that the tenth commandment
for marriage may have been
written as follows: You should
love your neighbour as yourself,
and especially your closest
"neighbour," your marriage partner.

INFIDELITY (204-209)

Today infidelity is running rampant, and we are all candidates for infidelity. When the escapade is finally over, all that is left is a feeling of shame – about the harm that we have caused by our infidelity, especially the harm to ourselves.

204

that fidelity means having secrets between
you that you may not share with
anyone else (and don't want to either).

205

that the temptation to be
unfaithful crosses everyone's
path – it even crossed the path
of God's main psalmist, David.

206

that temptation should be
resisted from the very first moment.

207

that the allurements of
an affair are jack-o'-lanterns
that are mistaken for stars.

<u>208</u>

that if you spend a quarter of the
energy on your marriage that
you would spend on an extramaritai
affair, your marriage will taste like
ice-cream with chocolate sauce.

<u>209</u>

that a marriage without love
leads to a love without marriage.

MATURITY (210-223)

*Actually marriage is only meant for mature
people. And we are all rather immature,
especially in our twenties. That is why each
one of us should work hard at leaving our
selfish childishness behind and growing up.*

210

that Hollywood has never understood
what love is, because if it did,
Elizabeth Taylor would not have
married nine times in search of it.

211

that change should start with yourself.

212

that seeking professional help with
your marriage is a sign of strength.

213

that cruelty is only found
in weak people, and that
tenderness is a sign of strength.

214

that happiness is a choice.

215

that nothing is always
altogether pleasant.

216

that an adult is someone who
excuses the shortcomings of
fellow travellers on the highway of life.

217

that a person's age, status,
influence and possessions
are still no guarantee of
his or her degree of maturity.

218

that the actual grounds for many
marital problems lie in the emotional
immaturity of one or even both parties.

219

that maturity is especially
situated in the fact that
you don't live according
to your feelings, but according
to your faith and that which is right.

220

that maturity means that you
don't keep on dreaming about
a utopia in the clouds, or an ideal
person in the milky way, but that
you make a success of this marriage,
with this partner, under these
circumstances, in this world.

<u>221</u>

that maturity means that you shouldn't
just look for a marriage partner under
the moon, but especially someone
who can live with you under the sun.

<u>222</u>

that emotionally mature people
accept themselves, other people
and especially the **one** person,
their marriage partner, and constantly
try to improve their relationship.

<u>223</u>

that maturity enables you to persevere
and hold on, keep your mouth
shut and your hands held tight,
stick it out and follow through.

NEEDS (224-236)

We all have many healthy needs which can only be satisfied by someone else. In a good marriage, marriage partners constantly strive to fulfil the needs of their partners. And the one who gives, usually receives as well.

224

that your greatest need can only
be fulfilled by another person.

225

that you obtain the most accurate
image of yourself through the reactions
you evoke from someone close to you.

226

that in order to be a complete
person, you must be able
to be your own unique self,
and have enough flexibility
to live happily with someone
else for the rest of your life.

227

that of all feelings
loneliness is the worst.

228

that in order to live happily, we
should above all have faith – something you can only develop within
a relationship with others, and
especially with one particular person.

229

that a relationship with
someone means having a
place where you are never alone.

230

that you don't need someone else
to tell you how you feel and
who you are, but someone who
can understand what you feel and
can accept who and what you are.

231

that if you have a need to receive love –
and it is the greatest need we all
experience! – you should give love.

232

that everyone needs at least one
person to whom he or she can reveal
that he or she is vulnerable and fragile
without losing his or her self-image.

233

how to move away from
competition towards co-operation.

234

that tears say something, con-
stitute a language, and that
men may also speak this language.

235

that you should devote at
least one weekend every
three months to each other only.

236

that true talent and personality can only come to the surface and develop within a relationship between marriage partners.

HUMOUR (237-246)

Man is the only creature God made that can laugh and smile, and man can smile because he knows that God exists, and no circumstance is greater than God.

237

that humour was born from the fact that God smiles a million times more about the future than what he frows about the past.

238

never to use humour to the detriment of your partner.

239

that you should tell your
partner the new joke first.

240

that women don't shave
because it would mean that
the jaw would have to be kept
motionless for at least four minutes.

241

that any man who thinks that he is
more intelligent than a woman is
married to a very intelligent woman.

242

that the purpose of being in love is
that it makes a man think just as
much of a girl as he does of himself.

243

that a man may not criticise his wife's mistakes, because without those mistakes she might have chosen a better man.

244

that if a man says that he's the boss in his home, he will lie about other things as well.

245

that a man may only speak with a full mouth if he wants to compliment his wife on her delicious food, which he is eating.

246

that the words "the writing on the
walls" could also mean that there
are small hands in the house
that have received crayons as a gift.

PRIORITIES (247-249)

*The happy and responsible person is the one
who always determines whether he places
emphasis on the right things, whether his
preferences are truly realistic, and who is
prepared to make adjustments.*

247

that God instituted marriage to teach
people to place the most important
things first – and that as long as you
still come first, you have not yet learnt
the Christian way of counting.

248

that your marriage requires
the best and not the rest.

249

that being a marriage partner
is permanent and being a
parent is only semi-permanent.

SIN (250-256)

*Many people think that sin is an obsolete
expression. That is how sinful we are, because
the second biggest reality in the life of every
person of every century is his or her sin. The
biggest? God's forgiveness.*

250

that you are also unfaithful to your
marriage partner with your bad attitude.

251

that clamming up is a sin,
and cannot at all be used as
an excuse to avoid arguments.

252

that not wanting to forgive your
marriage partner is just
as great a sin as that which
your partner has done wrong.

253

that there is probably no bigger
sin than marrying your partner
and then allowing him or her
to remain with you (in your sha-
dow), crumbling away without love.

254

that being dishonest with
your partner is an even bigger
sin than "ordinary" dishonesty.

255

that any kind of extramarital
relationship, or anything that can lead
to such a relationship, is and always will
be a sin – and can never be justified.

256

that whoever remains silent about
sin speaks the language of the devil.

THE SMALL THINGS (257-267)
*We are so inclined to think that the big things
really matter. Meanwhile life shows us that if
you keep the small things in good order, the
big things will almost look after themselves.*

257

that the small acts of consideration
are the oil that keeps the love-lamp
of our marriage burning brightly.

258

that you realise later on that if
you heed the small things, your
marriage means a lot more to
you than just a few small things.

259

that true love means that you
are even prepared to squeeze
the toothpaste from the other
side if that is what your partner wants.

260

that the whole issue of marriage is made up of the small things, like saying hello in the morning and goodnight in the evening, and really meaning it.

261

that "making love" actually means the small acts of consideration and empathy outside the bedroom.

262

that if you don't behave the same in your marriage than during your engagement, you are someone with double standards.

263

that it's the small bugs that destroy the
vineyard of marriage, but that it is also
the small dew drops that help the
vineyard to survive even the winter.

264

that celebrating your wedding anniversary really means that you are to
your partner every day that which you
promised to be on your wedding day.

265

that the more you do small
things for your partner, the smal-
ler your marital problems become.

266

that one of the surest ways to let a
relationship grow is eating together.

267

what the test of greatness is:
how you treat insignificant people.

QUARRELLING (268-273)
*All people quarrel! Christians discuss differences
calmly and solve their problems in a peaceful
manner.*

268

that you may never shout at each
other, unless the house is on fire.

269

that quarrelling only
causes hurt and solves nothing.

270

that if you quarrel, it means that you
want to have the last word – until the
last word one day becomes divorce.

271

that never quarrelling in your
marriage is not an illusion, but
a Christian possibility and reality.

272

that if a Christian couple cannot live
in peace and harmony, we may as
well build prisons where we now have
churches and schools and cultural centres.

273

that never quarrelling does not
mean that there aren't any
differences and misunderstandings,
and that things that make you
angry will never occur – but these
things should be talked through
with great patience and indulgence.

AGE (274-286)

*Marriage doesn't grow old as the years go by,
it only becomes deeper, more comfortable,
more mature and more loving. That is to say,
if marriage partners reach out and accept each
other more and more with renewed fervour.*

274

that we are all growing older, but
that it's no tragedy, because
despite that which a person loses
due to age, there is also so much
we gain – and that a person can be
happy until his or her very last breath.

275

that one gradually becomes more
and more what you are – that is why
you should work on yourself from
an early age, in order to already start
changing – and thus you can grow old
differently from what you really were.

276

that you should work at your relationship,
so that when the children leave home, you
can enjoy communicating with each
other – and not try to steal each other's
moisture like two dried-up old trees.

277

that people who are happy in their old
age are those who do not allow themselves
to be typified according to their losses
and the mistakes they have made, but
according to how (through the Lord's
mercy) they have changed and developed.

~ ☺ ~

<u>278</u>

that we ought to take care that we will have reserves – financially, socially, emotionally and especially spiritually – to draw from in our old age.

<u>279</u>

that a man is hard but breakable, and a woman is soft but durable. Therefore we need each other in our old age, even more than before.

<u>280</u>

that you really ought to renew your marriage vows with a service in church followed by a ceremony at home, and a second honeymoon. Because even the most beautiful wood can only benefit from a new layer of varnish.

~ 9·9 ~

281

that even if your hands become shaky,
they can still touch; that even if you
don't remember everything anymore,
you must never forget to comfort;
that even if you become sensitive
to cold, you can still cherish your
partner in the warmth of your love.

282

that love may not retire or become arthritic.

283

that the older your partner
becomes, the younger you
should make him or her feel.

284

that your skin may wrinkle,
but never your soul or your
enthusiasm or your love.

285

that the secret to happiness is counting
your blessings, and not your birthdays.

286

that the nicest thing about
growing old is that you don't
have to worry about it anymore.

DIVORCE (287-296)

*Divorce is not part of marriage. It is always
unnecessary. But it is relevant here because a
divorced person may never be judged.*

287

that divorce is one of the most
far-reaching traumas for the one
who doesn't want to get divorced.

288

that there is already grounds
for divorce within the first week
of marriage, but that the secret
is seeking – and finding –
more and more grounds for
staying married until our deathbed.

289

that the word "divorce" should
be cut out of your marriage
vocabulary, because you shouldn't
even consider it as a possibility.

290

that a person doesn't try out a marriage, but makes a marriage work.

291

that it should be one of the ten commandments of our marriage never to threaten to leave each other.

292

that marriage partners should write the words of God, "Behold, I make all things new," above their marriage and believe in this.

293

that there are more divorced people than those who appear in front of a judge.

294

that children should at all times and at
all costs be sure that their divorcing parents are not divorcing them.

295

if you could not make a success of
your marriage, you should at least try
to make a success of your divorce;
that means not being bitter or re-
proachful and not using your children
as pawns to get at your ex-partner.

296

that when parents get divorced, they
should at all costs insulate their
children against their own pain and
their anger towards their ex-partner.

WILL OUR MARRIAGE LAST? (297-310)
In the light of the high divorce rate, it is a natural question to ask. If, however, you fulfil the small duties that marriage requires, and make the small sacrifices, you can be certain: your marriage will definitely last.

297

that happily married
people really do exist.

298

that instead of trying to change
the world, one should rather
create a place for yourself in
it where you can live happily.

299

that a relationship lives or dies to
the extent that it receives attention.

300

that marriage requires that,
now that you have made your
choice, you no longer seek someone who might please you, but
that you constantly seek to
please the one that you have chosen.

301

that there are quite a number of tests
that you can subject yourself to in order
to determine whether your marriage
will last – of which the first is the
transparency test: whether you open
up your life to your partner, and not
carry around a lot of secrets within you.

302

that the second test could be the space test: whether you constantly work at giving your partner the space and freedom he needs within your relationship to develop into the person God intended him or her to be.

303

that the third test could be the unselfishness test: whether you are working strongly at recognising and acknowledging your own selfishness, and gradually trying to minimise it, thus allowing your partner to become more important than yourself.

304

that the fourth test is the forgiveness
test: whether you are already capable
of finally forgiving your partner's small
and large irritations and mistakes.

305

that the fifth test could be the
apology test: whether you are
prepared to apologise sincerely
for what you have done and still do.

306

that the sixth test can be called
the sex test: whether you have
reached the point where your
partner has become more important
than your own desires and needs.

307

that the seventh could be the financial
test: whether your love has reached
as far as your purse, and whether you have placed your marriage
above your stinginess or extravagance.

308

that the eighth, the pleasure test, asks
whether you have learnt to sometimes
really enjoy something small that
you experience or do, particularly
because you partner enjoys it so much.

309

that the ninth test is the jealousy test:
whether you have already recognised
your selfish jealousy (placing
your partner in a spot and being
unnecessarily suspicious of him or her)
and have started to overcome this.

310

that the tenth test should be the faith test: whether you have given yourself to the Lord in such a way that you can help to make your marriage work through his grace.

MONEY (311-316)

Marriage is also concerned with material things, with money. This has caused many marriages to end. That is why you should in this regard make unselfish arrangements together, and serve each other with your rands and cents as well.

311

that it always pays the highest interest if both partners know everything about each other's finances.

<u>312</u>

that throwing your money
together saves a lot of
money and time and arguments.

<u>313</u>

that even if only one of the two
earns the money, the other one
enables that one to do it – therefore that money is shared money.

<u>314</u>

that the one who doesn't earn hard
cash still contributes the "software"
of assistance and support, comfort
and help, acceptance and inspiration.

315

that you may even bank at two
different banks if that works out
better for the two of you – as long
as you pray beside the same bed.

316

that both should have some money
at their disposal for which no account
or explanations have to be given.

FLEXIBILITY (317-325)

*It is good, and sometimes necessary also to
have (unwritten) rules and regulations for your
marriage. But because people are involved,
the rules have to be flexible, and only the love
inflexible and unbreakable.*

317

that your love shouldn't be
cast iron which cannot break,
but steel which is flexible and
ductile and supple and can yield –
when circumstances require it to.

318

that love is being willing
to make compromises so that
every situation is a win-win one.

319

that only a statue has a point
on which it can always stand, but
that the Lord (whose grace is new
every morning) may ask us to be
or do something new tomorrow.

320

that the trees that are
rooted the deepest can bend
with the storm – and survive.

321

that even if you feel you will
die if you have to do something particular, you still
manage to do it (without dying!)
if love requires you to do it.

322

that it is the one who can
bend forward and backward, and
stretch and shrink for the sake
of his or her marriage partner,
who has unbendable principles.

<u>323</u>

that it is sometimes necessary to abandon your principles – and to do what is right.

<u>324</u>

that love is really the only
principle you may have.

<u>325</u>

that you should allow for your
children to fail, and that you
shouldn't fail them when they have failed.

COMPANIONSHIP (326-333)

*In marriage husband and wife are on exactly
the same, equal level. On that level they should
be friends. A person is, however, only a friend
if he works hard at becoming one.*

326:

that every good marriage
should also mean friendship.

327

that companionship and friendship
mean that part of another person
lives within you – like a sympa-
thetic voice that comforts you –
inspires you and always reminds
you of the unique bond between you.

328

that a companion and friend
is a place where you can
go in search of yourself.

329

that a true friend is someone who
accepts you wholeheartedly, and
doesn't wait for something to happen
which will make the friendship essential.

330

that you are a friend if your partner feels happier in your presence.

331

that getting closer to someone
is more important than receiving
400 Christmas cards every year.

332

that you may not judge your partner
before you have walked through the
snow for two weeks in his or her shoes.

333

that friendship is something
that should constantly be
spruced up, healed and oiled.

HONESTY (334-343)

*You can only be honest in your life if you
become honest in your marriage. Dishonesty
makes everything in marriage unsure and
destroys it. Honesty and fidelity enhance and
preserve your marriage.*

334

that blatant honesty can sometimes be harmful – especially
when it is used to cause hurt.

335

that very few other things keep a
relationship safer than the realisation
and decision that it is based on honesty.

336

that if you aren't honest, you cannot
love either – except if your love
for your partner should rather
make you remain silent sometimes.

337

that the most dangerous
of all lies is the deadly truth.

338

that you cannot live without cau-
sing your partner pain, but
that love can forgive pain, make
it fade and eventually disappear.

339

that the truth can injure temporarily,
but that a lie leaves permanent scars.

340

that nobody is always honest, and that you mostly lie in order to protect yourself.

341

that no one admits to something unless he is granted the freedom to move on without fear; if not so he will continue defending things he might not even really believe in.

342

that the sign of the church is a dove, not a chameleon; it starts in your marriage.

343

that your marriage starts working as soon as you become truly honest with yourself and with your partner.

ALCOHOL (344-353)
Abuse of liquor and divorce often go hand in hand. A mature view of alcohol is necessary for a mature way of living.

344

that Scripture also speaks positively about wine (e.g. Lev. 23:13, Song 5:1, Mt. 9:17) and that total abstinence does not have to be the only view with regard to liquor.

345

that the Bible warns against alcohol (e.g. Gen. 9:21, Rom. 14:21) and that it is foolish not to heed these warnings.

346

alcohol has most probably destroyed more lives and marriages and people than any other wretchedness on earth.

347

that the problem with alcohol is that it
makes you do things while you are
not completely aware of enjoying it –
and that it is therefore very sober to
stick to the rule: I never abuse
alcohol, because I want to be fully
aware of it when I am enjoying something.

348

that alcohol as such is not
sinful, but that you sin with it
as soon as you have to drink.

349

that a person should also be
able to celebrate something
without alcohol – if that's not possible you have mixed up your priorities.

350

that people with a drinking problem deny
that there is a problem, are convinced that
they can solve the problem on their own
– and meanwhile are just further caught
up in the octopus tentacles of alcohol.

351

that an alcoholic is not only the
person who regularly lies drunk
on the street, but anyone who
experiences problems (no matter
how small) in his or her relationships with people due to alcohol.

352

that some people are simply not
physically able to use alcohol without
being changed radically by it or being
caught up in the clutches of it, and
therefore they have to make the small
sacrifice of cutting it out of their lives.

353

that if you aren't prepared to make this sacrifice, it should convince you that alcohol completely impairs your insight.

DEATH (354-365)

Death is part of life, in the sense that it is the temporary end of life. Therefore we should take it into account. However, fortunately we can also thank God that it's also the beginning of eternal life.

354

love is always here and now. Even the memory of a deceased loved one is here and now – it is just continued in silence.

355

that the meaning of a relationship is sometimes only understood once it is over.

356

that death is just as certain as life.

357

that the day will come when
one of us will help to bury the
other – if we don't die together.

358

that you will keep on missing
your partner long after the day
that your friends feel you should
start ending your mourning period.

359

that reality requires that you make the
necessary financial and other practical
preparations – so that the surviving spouse
should not have to bear the extra burden.

360

that you should draw up a testament
directly after your wedding, even if
you only have yourselves to bequeath.

361

that because Christ killed death, death
in the marriage doesn't mean death
(and the death of everything) anymore.

362

that it isn't selfish to pray that your
partner should remain spared for you
for a long time, and that in your
marriage you may see the
grandchildren of your children.

363

that the absence of someone
is just like the heavens – it
stretches over everything.

364

that the mercy of God is like
the sun that shines all over
and even when there are clouds,
and even when it is night, will
soon rise over everyone once again.

365

that the last word doesn't belong to death, but to the Prince
of life who turned death into the
final gateway through which we
gain entrance to life – eternal life.